FOR THE ANIMAL

FOR THE ANIMAL

JOSHUA POTEAT

NEW MICHIGAN PRESS
TUCSON, ARIZONA

NEW MICHIGAN PRESS
DEPT OF ENGLISH, P. O. BOX 210067
UNIVERSITY OF ARIZONA
TUCSON, AZ 85721-0067

<http://newmichiganpress.com/nmp>

Orders and queries to nmp@thediagram.com.

Copyright © 2013 by Joshua Poteat.
All rights reserved.

ISBN 978-1-934832-42-9. FIRST PRINTING.

Printed in the United States of America.

Design by Ander Monson.

Cover by Sarah Goldstein, "Untitled (Rider 1)," ink on paper, cast shadow, digital photography, 2008, dimensions variable. Frontispiece based on original art by Sarah Goldstein.

CONTENTS

For the Animal   1

Notes   21

Acknowledgments   23

I send a message by a Mouth that cannot speak.

—Lucie Brock-Broido

For Allison

FOR THE ANIMAL

For the animal goes from the house to the field in phases.
For the animal gives us a way to reason with God.
For the animal was a communication and is now a shroud.
For the animal takes depths to its shins and cuts the terror.
For the animal is a language of adversary.
For the animal meets another animal with duty/living light/
   seven folds against the dunes.
For the animal awakened, unnatural, failed to love.
For the animal by candlelight washes electric through the storm.
For the animal is ghost, monster and truce.

For the animal in snow chooses what to fear.

For the animal pulls glass from her sleeping foot, golden as fog.

For the animal volunteers its illegible years to live inside the river.

For the animal manufactures the day.

For the animal there are flowers of purpose in death.

For the animal is not ancient.

For the animal is not accident.

For the animal chooses what pain to protect.

For the animal's labor calls above the drought-lake.

For the animal in drink-machine light chooses the Diet Pepsi.
For the animal faxes flood insurance to the cattail grove.
For the animal shops for headstones online and gets a good deal.
For the animal wears a human face inside the silo.
For the animal watches humans circle the farmhouse well.
For the animal pulls from the taxidermy an arsenic shawl.
For the animal drapes the morning with an arsenic shawl.
For the animal refuses a glass of water from the sheriff's wife.
For the animal loves the sheriff.

For the animal bends into the creek in error, locks the briar,
> narrow crown of months tumble apart in the formaldehyde.

For the animal lives down the hall from the drink machine.
For the animal embezzling funds — there is no escape.
For the animal's narrative shows in tidal pools.
For the animal signals the machine with its one good eye.
For the animal speaks through its knife by trophy and landscape.
For the animal fragments itself on the electric fence.
For the animal is grotesque at the tobacco field's edge.
For the animal in black needlerush pulls apart the century.

For the animal creates itself on the asphalt trail.
For the animal creates itself in the truck-lot ditch.
For the animal creates itself by the factory's break room.
For the animal creates itself through the stomach of its child.
For the animal creates itself before the human birth.
For the animal creates itself covered in Saran wrap.
For the animal creates itself through mold and guile.
For the animal invented Old Norse to abate the coming winter.
For the animal floods the field with milk shapes.

For the animal regrets what makes looking possible.
For the animal is destined to petition the dried blood of day.
For the animal is adored and collects skins of the animal.
For the animal is obsessed and kills time with the animal.
For the animal eradicates the eternal.
For the animal hums at the blossom.
For the animal is unpleasant in the marsh and the salt that clings.
For the animal binds us to our boyhood sickness.
For the animal holds the nail gun against the rotted foot.

For the animal removes its wig to show its useful home.
For the animal in bed eating chips doesn't remember you at all.
For the animal is far away, moving among the statues.
For the animal forms a song on its teeth and it sounds like sleep.
For the animal wears the laughing gas suit.
For the animal takes field notes in the vacant house—there is a coastline nearby, a heron tendon-soft, a window closes on the wind's marrowed hand.
For the animal is a white sheet drawn behind the objects.
For the animal waves to us from across the years.
For the animal groups the Civil War widows by the amount of shrapnel in their bouquets.

For the animal in the garden of brokenness heals.

For the animal is recognized as the animal, a force like water, an artificial thing.

For the animal is whiteness on the horizon, reduced.

For the animal is observable in the wake of ships.

For the animal sets its bed under glass as though it had been living.

For the animal corked in rosin stops the progress of evil.

For the animal arranges its skin as if still awake.

For the animal encounters no barrier in its invisibility.

For the animal as souvenir gives voice to grief, to the sun that lights it.

For the animal in the abandoned house is worthy in its petition
   to endure.
For the animal violates the blood it is given near the yards and
   highways.
For the animal presses its face against the glass of summer.
For the animal tears away the slaughter.
For the animal in the GEICO commercial glows blue with heat.
For the animal at the keyboard cherishes what is no longer.
For the animal is the absence of the marvelous child.
For the animal is the marvelous child at the quarry's edge.
For the animal is the original violence.

For the animal swims the quarry in child clothes.
For the animal hides the seams to keep the suit authentic.
For the animal is witness to the disaster.
For the animal tells a story to itself about itself.
For the animal is someone else's souvenir.
For the animal's usefulness is exhausted.
For the animal is frustrated by the failure of the Dallas Cowboys.
For the animal is frustrated by the failure of the afterlife.
For the animal in the mirror translates the cicada husk.

For the animal and human overlap where silt meets iris stiffened
   to lung.
For the animal takes silence from the milk.
For the animal takes milk from the poor.
For the animal is grub-strung—its hunger lifts the rotted log.
For the animal's mouth will be the mouth of those griefs that
   have no mouth.
For the animal's honeyed eye collides with the dawn.
For the animal is belly-swell, is flood-face, is brackish-tooth, is
   there.
For the animal is docile and can learn certain things.
For the animal surveys the atmosphere from a ladder of
   withering blood.

For the animal was a girl once and was afraid.

For the animal was a dead man in the sweet-gum tree.

For the animal's affliction is unreliable and coats the grass like arms, like wind.

For the animal transmits its grievances on the black sound of lice.

For the animal remembers evil and sends out fires that are very like stars.

For the animal in 1900 taps on the window to test its muscle against life.

For the animal is a godless brother sleeping in your garage.

For the animal rubs its money cup on the amputee's wheelchair.

For the animal's room ails, hymn-to-hymn, graffiti on the bridge-sway, a tourniquet.

For the animal hires drug dogs to lick the blood from its eyes.
For the animal swells and flattens.
For the animal can give to a mute fish the notes of a nightingale.
For the animal on brackish water troubles through the plastic tide.
For the animal confesses its pink lungs to the frost.
For the animal hollows a flute for the wind.
For the animal was here, and will come again.
For the animal in cul-de-sac dark sentinels the birch.
For the animal dies for you in several ways.

For the animal lives inside another animal and there is nothing
    we can do.
For the animal is not dead—it lives in us by poverty and sun.
For the animal envies the tall grass on the interstate median—
    it lives for no one.
For the animal comes back as old hatred, winter moonlight on
    the dunes.
For the animal is brutal in its memory—its secret body rages
    under the field.
For the animal is conditional—it is not our silence to know.
For the animal has no name for "animal"—what a strange thing
    to say.
For the animal goes on to find the wilderness, to visit the place
    where names burst like clouds.
For the animal did not notice the stillness until the pines went
    black.

For the animal is a loneliness, and like all lonelinesses, rests in
    the Museum of Rope.
For the animal is surprised to be alive.
For the animal replaces abundance with Klonopin.
For the animal flickers in the alley among the red cans.
For the animal empties the trees with buckshot.
For the animal makes a wreath from 12-gauge cartridges.
For the animal in your childhood makes the wrong irredeemable.
For the animal does not forgive the childhoods.
For the animal is the absence of the stubborn world.

For the animal it is not grief that works: grief keeps watch.
For the animal drags its wing along the chain-link fence.
For the animal does not belong to death—it assumes suffering is natural.
For the animal tries to understand the sound of whiteness over the city.
For the animal buries stolen bread under the couch cushion.
For the animal is transparent against the floodwall ruin.
For the animal's citizenship is revoked, solemnly and with great sincerity.
For the animal crosses the county line out by the old lumberyard and does not look back at the falling snow.
For the animal creeks the trap, slantwise, locked by copse, by hollow.

For the animal is sleepy-time, is bye-bye, is numb-knees, is jewel-weed, is sorry.

For the animal can take the face out of the lake but not the lake out of the face.

For the animal leads the doe through the blizzard, gunnysack and all.

For the animal unsettles the hatchlings from lavender's ash trap.

For the animal mimeographs pin bones & ice fish & pine-leaf… wind…& star.

For the animal's apparatus measures light pollution, the sound of whiteness over the city.

For the animal tunnels lichen from the lantern's sad rain.

For the animal's evening thaws enough to break the interstate, one new widow in fever.

For the animal mourns the invention of suburbs, lamb-like in the stalls, crickets crushed between bales.

For the animal is uninspired, yawns over the doe-bed in
    honey-faced light.
For the animal's fish-scrawl cuffs the snow at sea.
For the animal is maybe a music ailing past dawn into the
    smallest white source.
For the animal, wounded, runs the tree-line mathematics.
For the animal wrings out its t-shirt, the river in fog, the
    bricks pleat in a drywall pile, worm-sick, appeased.
For the animal mosquitoes the veil, reblooms the air, sorts
    through the hailstones for the right twilight.
For the animal comforts no moon, breathes the wood-smoke
    meadow.
For the animal bears what you cannot.
For the animal thought you would never ask.

NOTES

…will be the mouth of those griefs that have no mouth.
Aime Cesaire

…is docile and can learn certain things.
Christopher Smart

…can give to a mute fish the notes of a nightingale.
Christopher Smart

…it is not grief that works: grief keeps watch.
Maurice Blanchot

…can take the face out of the lake but not the lake out of the face.
Julia Cohen

…pin bones & ice fish & pine-leaf…wind…& star.
Ann Marshall

…a white sheet drawn behind the objects.
John Constable

ACKNOWLEDGMENTS

Special thanks to my favorite animals:

Ander Monson, New Michigan Press, and *DIAGRAM*.
Christopher Smart and his cat Jeoffry for *Jubilate Agno*, the
    text *For the Animal* is based on.
Rachel Polinquin's book *The Breathless Zoo: Taxidermy and
    the Cultures of Longing*.
Dario Robleto's book *Alloy of Love*.
Sarah Goldie Goldstein for the beautiful cover art.
Jake Adam York, whose love of barbeque does not diminish
    my love for him.
Ann Marshall
Nancy Foltz/The Martin Agency for giving me an office on
    the 17th floor in which to complete this work and others.
And my most favorite animals of all: Allison, Ruben, Piper,
    Elly and Daisy.

COLOPHON

Text is set in a digital version of Jenson, designed by Robert Slimbach in 1996, and based on the work of punchcutter, printer, and publisher Nicolas Jenson.

JOSHUA POTEAT has published two books of poems, *Ornithologies* (Anhinga Poetry Prize, 2006) and *Illustrating the Machine that Makes the World* (*VQR*/University of Georgia Press, 2009), as well as a chapbook, *Meditations* (Poetry Society of America, 2004). A chapbook, *The Scenery of Farewell (and Hello Again)*, is forthcoming from Diode Editions, 2014. Originally from Hampstead, North Carolina, he lives in Richmond, Virginia, with the writer Allison Titus and their four dogs.

NEW MICHIGAN PRESS, based in Tucson, Arizona, prints poetry and prose chapbooks, especially work that transcends traditional genre. Together with DIAGRAM, NMP sponsors a yearly chapbook competition.

DIAGRAM, a journal of text, art, and schematic, is published bimonthly at THEDIAGRAM.COM. Periodic print anthologies are available from the New Michigan Press at NEWMICHIGANPRESS.COM/NMP.

www.ingramcontent.com/pod-product-compliance
Lightning Source LLC
Chambersburg PA
CBHW031508040426
42444CB00007B/1248